GALE
CENGAGE Learning

Drama for Students, Volume 6

Staff

Editorial: David M. Galens, *Editor*. Tim Akers, *Contributing Editor*. James Draper, *Managing Editor*. David Galens and Lynn Koch, *"For Students" Line Coordinators*. Jeffery Chapman, *Programmer/Analyst*.

Research: Victoria B. Cariappa, *Research Manager*. Andrew Guy Malonis, Barbara McNeil, Gary J. Oudersluys, Maureen Richards, and Cheryl L. Warnock, *Research Specialists*. Patricia Tsune Ballard, Wendy K. Festerling, Tamara C. Nott, Tracie A. Richardson, Corrine A. Stocker, and, Robert Whaley, *Research Associates*. Phyllis J. Blackman, Tim Lehnerer, and Patricia L. Love, *Research Assistants*.

Permissions: Maria Franklin, *Permissions Manager*. Kimberly F. Smilay, *Permissions Specialist*. Kelly A. Quin, *Permissions Associate*. Sandra K. Gore,

Permissions Assistant.

Graphic Services: Randy Bassett, *Image Database Supervisor*. Robert Duncan and Michael Logusz, *Imaging Specialists*. Pamela A. Reed, *Imaging Coordinator*. Gary Leach, *Macintosh Artist*.

Product Design: Cynthia Baldwin, *Product Design Manager*. Cover Design: Michelle DiMercurio, *Art Director*. Page Design: Pamela A. E. Galbreath, *Senior Art Director*.

Copyright Notice

of this work have added value to the underlying factual material herein through one or more of the following: unique and original selection, coordination, expression, arrangement, and classification of information. All rights to this publication will be vigorously defended.

This book is printed on acid-free paper that meets the minimum requirements of American National Standard for Information Sciences—Permanence Paper for Printed Library Materials, ANSI Z39.48-1984.

ISBN 0-7876-2755-0
ISSN 1094-9232

Printed in the United States of America
10 9 8 7 6 5 4 3

Hedda Gabler

Henrik Ibsen

1890

Introduction

Hedda Gabler, published in 1890, was first performed in Munich, Germany, on January 31, 1891, and over the next several weeks was staged in a variety of European cities, including Berlin, Stockholm, Copenhagen, and Christiania (Oslo). Its premier performance in English occurred in London, on April 20 of the same year, in a translation by Edmund Gosse and William Archer (a translation that has continued to be employed throughout the twentieth century).

Many scholars link the play with what Ibsen described as the happiest event in his life, his brief liaison with Emilie Bardach, an eighteen-year-old Viennese girl whom he met in the small Alpine town of Gossensass in September of 1889. It is an ironic association, for in the months after the sixty-two-year old playwright stopped corresponding with Emilie, he wrote *Hedda Gabler*, which Herman Weigand termed the "coldest, most impersonal of Ibsen's plays" in *The Modern Ibsen: A Reconsideration*. It is almost as though the normally reserved and distant Ibsen had to exorcize his emotional attachment to Emilie by struggling to become yet more detached and objective in his art.

In its printed version, even before production, *Hedda Gabler* received the worst reviews of any of Ibsen's mature plays. Its earliest stagings fared little better. Conservative critics, predominately males, condemned the work as immoral, just as they had condemned many of Ibsen's earlier social-problem plays. It survived the critical deluge, however, thanks in no small part to the efforts of the dramatist's ardent admirers, many of whom—including playwright George Bernard Shaw—belonged to the new intelligentsia shaped by the revolutionary thinking of such philosophers and scientists as Karl Marx and Charles Darwin.

Hedda Gabler's reputation steadily rose in the twentieth century, engaging the interest of many important actresses who found in Hedda one of the most intriguing and challenging female roles in modern drama. They helped earn the play the eminence it now enjoys as one of Ibsen's premier works and a landmark of realist drama.

Author Biography

At the time Henrik Ibsen wrote and published *Hedda Gabler* (1890) he was sixty-two and a well-established but highly controversial dramatist, but the road to that success had been paved with deprivation and hardship. Although he was born in a well-to-do family in Skien, Norway, on March 20, 1828, financial reversals led to poverty, making Henrik's youth a dismal one. At sixteen, he began a lonely and unhappy six-year apprenticeship to an apothecary (a pharmacist). He found his principal solace in the theater and writing, which he hoped would provide a means of escaping from his misery.

His first serious attempt at drama, *Cataline* (1850), earned him the support of friends who helped him escape from drudgery. He moved to Christiania (Oslo), where he undertook an apprenticeship as dramatist with the Bergen National Theatre. He also spent time in Copenhagen, studying at the Royal Theatre.

Ibsen's first plays borrowed freely from the French intrigue drama that he derided for its artificiality. Hoping to write something new, in 1857 he left the Bergen Theatre to become the director of the Norwegian Theatre in Christiania. The next year, despite his wretched financial state, he married and began a family. Nothing seemed to go right, however. His plays and poetry gained no influential following, and his theater went bankrupt within five years.

Lack of public support forced him into exile. In 1864, he moved to Rome. It was the first major turning point in his long career, for it was as an expatriate that he wrote most of the plays on which his great international reputation was built. Not only did he leave Scandinavia, he left behind a direct participation in theater. While in Italy, he wrote *Brand* (1866) and *Peer Gynt* (1867), two important poetic dramas. The former play was an immediate success and helped alleviate Ibsen's dire poverty.

In 1868, the French invasion of Italy obliged Ibsen to move to Germany, where he began writing the series of plays on which his fame largely rests. He turned from writing mythic-poetic drama to realistic, social-problem drama in prose, starting with *The League of Youth* in 1869, which, like so many of its successors, caused an uproar when first staged. Although his success was limited, by the time he returned to Rome in 1878, he had permanently freed himself from debt.

In the next year, 1879, he published *A Doll's House*, garnering international acclaim and putting him, critically, at center stage. Each succeeding social-thesis play brought increased recognition and notoriety, for each was, in some quarters, condemned. For example, *Ghosts* (1881) created such a furor that it could not be staged immediately. Others, like *An Enemy of the People* (1883) and *The Wild Duck* (1885), though less sensational, still caused critical controversy. Ibsen's fame and his notoriety spread quickly.

By 1890, when *Hedda Gabler* was published, he had even become a national hero in Norway. He returned home in 1891, where, before his death, he wrote *The Master Builder* (1892), *Little Eyolf* (1894), *John Gabriel Borkman* (1896), and *When We Dead Awaken* (1899), dramas that are more symbolic and introspective than any of his previous works. He died on May 23, 1906, widely regarded as the most important dramatist of the age.

Act I

Hedda Gabler opens in the drawing room of the Tesmans' villa in the prestigious west-end district of Christiania, Norway. George Tesman and his new wife, Hedda, have just returned from a six-month honeymoon. Juliana Tesman, George's maiden aunt, and Berta, the Tesmans' servant, talk about George's invalid Aunt Rina, Hedda's father, General Gabler, and George's fortunate marriage and bright career prospects.

George enters, greets his aunt, and sends Berta off to store his valise while he helps Juliana remove her new bonnet. They discuss his good fortune in winning the much-admired Hedda, who, Juliana hopes, may already be pregnant. The journey and the villa and its furnishings, arranged by Judge Brack, have put both George and his aunts in debt, but Juliana assures her nephew that he is sure to get his anticipated academic appointment. Eilert Lovborg, George's chief competitor for the position, remains in disgrace, despite his popular new book.

When Hedda enters, she is both brusque and ill-mannered. After implying that Juliana's visit is too early, she complains about the room's stuffiness. She refuses to take any interest in George's favorite slippers, newly embroidered by his invalid aunt, and declares that Berta will have to be discharged for carelessly leaving her old bonnet on a chair. She also gets annoyed with George when he talks of her robust health, of how she seems to have "filled out" on their journey.

When George sees his aunt to the door, Hedda reveals her mounting frustration and rage by raising clenched fists over her head. He returns and they talk briefly about Aunt Juliana and Hedda's refusal to become closer to her. Berta then shows in Mrs. Elvsted, who explains that Eilert Lovborg is in town; she implores the Tesmans to befriend him. After Hedda sends George off to write Lovborg an amiable letter, she begins grilling Thea about her marriage to Sheriff Elvsted and her relationship to Lovborg. Accepting Hedda's apparent friendship, Thea confides that she has helped reform the dissolute Lovborg. She also confesses that she has left her husband, but that Lovborg has not encouraged her feelings for him because he remains emotionally bound to a former lover who had once driven him away at gunpoint.

George returns to find that they have another visitor, Judge Brack. After introductions, Hedda sees Thea out and returns to find the men talking about Lovborg, his book, and his moral reclamation. Brack then tells George that his academic appointment is not a certainty, that there is to be a competition for the post, pitting him against Lovborg—this news greatly upsets the financially-strapped Tesman. He voices his concerns to Hedda after Brack leaves, explaining that they will have to become much more frugal. She tells him that she will be bored but will amuse herself with her father's pistols.

Act II

It is late-afternoon on the same day. Judge Brack, approaching the Tesmans' villa from the rear, is dismayed when Hedda fires a pistol in his direction. After chiding her, Brack presses Hedda for a more intimate friendship. She reveals her disenchantment with marriage, complaining that the unexciting Tesman is simply too absorbed in his dull studies. She scoffs at the idea of love, admitting that she married George, not from affection, but because he is solid and respectable and has good prospects.

George enters laden with several books, one of which is Lovborg's new work. When he goes into the study, Hedda confesses her dislike for Tesman's aunts and even the married couple's villa. She admits she had only pretended to believe that Juliana's new bonnet belonged to Berta. She also tells Brack that she has hopes of interesting George in politics, but he offers no encouragement. His suggestion that she might find an alternative interest in raising a child makes her bristle.

When George re-enters, the talk turns to Lovborg and Judge Brack's bachelor's party. Shortly after, Eilert arrives, hoping to read part of his manuscript to George. He refuses an invitation to the party but defers to Hedda's insistence that he stay for dinner with her and Thea Elvsted. He also indicates that he will not stand in the way of Tesman's appointment, much to George's relief.

Lovborg stays alone with Hedda while the other men go into an adjoining room to drink punch. They speak of their former intimacy, of a time when Eilert confided in her. She confesses that she dreads the scandal that their love might have occasioned, a fear she still carries. He then allays her concern by revealing that he has never told Thea of their love, that Thea was too stupid to understand it.

When Mrs. Elvsted arrives, she tells Hedda of her happiness in being a catalyst in Lovborg's moral and professional reformation. Hedda suggests that Eilert is not really very secure, that both he and others, including Brack, suspect a possible relapse. She then betrays Thea's trust by revealing to Lovborg that Thea had come to her in a distracted state, herself fearful of what Eilert might do. To Thea's chagrin, Lovborg reacts bitterly, resolving to go off to the party with Tesman and Brack, with plans to read his manuscript there.

The men depart, leaving the worried Thea and exultant Hedda alone. Hedda is convinced that Eilert will return "with vine-leaves in his hair." She admits that she desires the power to shape one person's destiny, and, reverting to a girlhood threat, says that she will yet have to burn the frightened Thea's hair off. At the curtain, she restates her conviction that Eilert will return in all his vine-leaf (drunken and disorderly) glory.

Act III

It is early the following day. Hedda and Thea have spent the night awaiting the return of Lovborg and Tesman. Hedda is asleep on the sofa, but Thea, restless, merely dozes in a chair. She wakes fully when Berta enters with a letter for George. Hedda also wakes, and after allaying Thea's concern, sends her off to rest in another room.

When Tesman returns, he tells Hedda that Lovborg had read part of his new manuscript to him and that is an extraordinary work. He also reveals that he has the manuscript with him, that he picked it up after Eilert carelessly dropped it, something only George knows. Hedda insists that he leave it with her. He is hesitant, but when he learns from the letter that his Aunt Rina is dying, he prepares to go to his aunt's bedside. Hedda stashes the manuscript out of sight, on the bookcase, just before Brack enters.

Brack describes Lovborg's behavior of the previous night, of how the scholar had gone to Mademoiselle Diana's room, charged everyone with stealing his papers, and, after striking a constable, been taken to jail. Eilert's fate comforts Brack, who had seen Lovborg as a threat to his plans to ensnare Hedda in an intimate relationship.

After Brack leaves, Hedda takes the packet of Lovborg's papers from the bookcase, but hearing voices in the hall, locks them in the drawer of a writing table. Lovborg barges in over the protests of Berta. Shortly after, Mrs. Elvsted also enters, and he tells her that she must leave him and go home again, that he is ruined. He lies to her, claiming to have torn his manuscript to pieces, scattering it on the fjord. She exits in despair, blaming Lovborg for destroying their work, their "child."

After Thea's exit, Eilert tells Hedda the truth, that he has lost the manuscript, and that he plans "to make an end of all." Hedda then begs him to end it "beautifully," and gives him one of General Gabler's pistols. After he leaves, she retrieves his manuscript and destroys it in the drawing room's stove.

Act IV

It is evening of the same day. Juliana talks of her sister's death with Hedda and George. She announces her desire to find another invalid to nurse, then adds the hope that Hedda will also have another to care for, a baby. After Juliana leaves, Hedda confesses that she had burned Eilert's manuscript to ashes. George is horrified, but when she claims that she did it for his sake, and lets on that she is with child, his regret turns to joy, and he agrees that they should keep her destruction of Eilert's papers a secret.

Mrs. Elvsted then joins them. She has heard rumors that Eilert was taken to the hospital. These are soon confirmed by Judge Brack, who enters shortly after. He claims that Eilert is in the hospital, dying from a self-inflicted gunshot wound in the chest, news that only slightly distresses Hedda, who had expected him to shoot himself "beautifully," in the temple. When the talk shifts to Lovborg's destroyed manuscript, Thea suggests that from notes she has with her, she and Tesman might be able to recreate Eilert's work. George is at once enthusiastic, and the pair go into an adjoining room to begin what George now perceives as his life's work.

Alone with Hedda, Brack tells her the truth about Lovborg, that he is already dead, having bled to death from a wound to his bowels accidentally inflicted while Eilert was with Mademoiselle Diana in her boudoir. George then re-enters to say that he wants to work with Thea at the writing table. Hedda, after covering the remaining pistol with music sheets, moves apart, continuing her conversation with Brack *sotto voce* ("under the voice," in drama, a whispering technique that allows an audience to hear the dialogue). He reveals that he recognized the pistol that Lovborg used and warns her that a scandal could follow were he to disclose what he knows. She realizes what he is insinuating, that Eilert's death and her fear of scandal will put her completely in Brack's power.

As Thea and George work on Eilert's notes, Hedda goes into the adjoining room with music sheets and the pistol. She begins frenzied playing on the piano, prompting Tesman to protest the music's inappropriateness, given the death of Rina. George also tells Thea that they should work at Juliana's house in the evenings, leaving Brack to keep Hedda company. Brack is immediately agreeable, knowing that he can turn such occasions into sexual trysts. Hedda then fires the pistol, and when the men jump up and go into the room, they discover that Hedda has shot herself in the temple, something, according to the astonished Brack, that people just "don't do."

Berta

Berta is the Tesmans' middle-aged, maid. She is a loyal family retainer, formerly employed by George Tesman's maiden aunts but now in the service of George and Hedda at their newly purchased villa. Her closeness to Juliana Tesman makes her a minor threat to Hedda, who intensely dislikes George's aunt. Early on, Hedda threatens to discharge Berta, partly to discomfort George, but also because she clearly identifies Berta with George's family and its deeply affectionate binds that Hedda loathes. Although Berta appears often, she has no significant part in the play's action. She is very protective of George Tesman and his privacy.

Judge Brack

Judge Brack hides his desire for an intimate relationship with Hedda with an outward friendship for George Tesman and a cloak of respectability. He is, in truth, quite sinister and unprincipled, a sophisticated stalker who awaits an opportunity to seduce Hedda, to become the "one cock in the basket."

Brack is particularly dangerous because he is a fair judge of character, except, finally, in Hedda's case. He is genuinely shocked by her suicide, something he did not anticipate would result from his success in maneuvering her into a compromising position. He is otherwise a glib and masterful manipulator. At the outset, it is made clear that he has put George Tesman in his debt by arranging the loans for purchasing the villa. George, ingenuous to a fault, sees Brack only as an unselfish friend, one he trusts implicitly. Brack also challenges the hapless Lovborg, inviting him to his party, knowing full well that Eilert might slip again into his former dissolution. Hedda, on the other hand, penetrates Brack's mask of good will, identifying the leering innuendo in much of his seemingly harmless conversation with her.

It is Brack who forces Hedda into her last desperate act, her self-destruction. He knows that the pistol used by Eilert Lovborg was one of a pair of General Gabler's pistols in Hedda's possession. That he can expose her and subject her to scandal gives him the advantage he has sought, but Hedda, unwilling to become his "slave," elects to escape such a predicament through death.

Mrs. Elvsted

During the course of *Hedda Gabler*, Thea confesses that she has fled from her loveless and boorish husband, Sheriff Elvsted, and her stepchildren, destroying her reputation to follow Eilert Lovborg to Christiania. For the prior two years, she had both reformed the debauched

Lovborg and inspired his new work. Despite her great influence on the brilliant Eilert, her hopes of securing his love are faint. A shadow sits on their relationship: Eilert's residual feelings for a former lover, who, unbeknownst to Thea, is Hedda Gabler.

Thea and Hedda, like Eilert and George Tesman, are sharply contrasting characters. Thea has courage and hope, selflessness and warmth. She is willing to risk all for love, even the kind of scandal that cowers Hedda, and though she knows her love for Eilert Lovborg is futile, her chief concern is for him, not herself. Hedda, on the other hand, is selfish and severe, incapable of the generosity of spirit necessary to love.

The two women even contrast physically. Thea seems made of softer stuff, rounded, not chiseled like the obdurate, stone-cast Hedda. Both have a kind of beauty, but Thea's greater beauty lies within. It is reflected in her outer femininity, in her rich and luxuriant hair, particularly. Hedda's beauty is sharper, more masculine or androgynous.

Media Adaptations

- By the time film became commercially viable, Ibsen's reputation as one of the world's greatest dramatists was secure. In Europe and the United States, many early film directors tried their hand at adapting Ibsen's plays to the early cinema. *Hedda Gabler* was adapted to the silent screen at least three times: in the United States in 1917, by Frank Powell; in Italy in 1919, by Giovanni Pastrone; and in Germany in 1924, by Franz Eckstein.

- A 1963 British television version of *Hedda Gabler*, directed by Alex Segal, cast major film stars Ingrid Bergman as Hedda, Trevor Howard as Lovborg, Michael Redgrave as Tesman, and Ralph Richardson as Judge (Assesor) Brack.

- Another television version of the play was produced by the British Broadcasting Corporation (BBC-TV) in 1972. Directed by Waris Hussein, its cast includes Tom Bell, Ian McKellen, and Janet Suzman. A video version is available from Time-Life Multimedia in the United States.

- A film version of the Royal Shakespeare Company's stage production was released in the U. K. in 1975 under the title *Hedda*. Directed by Trevor Nunn, it features Glenda Jackson, Peter Eyre, Timothy West, Jennie Linden, and Patrick Stewart. It is generally available on video.

- In 1976, Films for the Humanities issued an educational film entitled *The Theatre of Social Problems: Ibsen, Hedda*, featuring an abridged version of the play, which, with commentary, runs 60 minutes. Produced by Harold Mantell, directed by Philip Hedley, and narrated by Irene Worth, its cast includes Darlene Johnson, Brian Protheroe, Rhys McConnochie, Sam Kelley, and Sara Stephenson. It is available in both video and 16 mm. formats from Films for the Humanities.

- Another British television version, directed by Deborah Warner, was first aired in 1993. The cast includes Fiona Shaw as Hedda, Nicholas Woodeson as Jorgen Tesman, Donal McCann as Judge Brack, Stephen Rea as Eilert Lovborg, Brid Brenan as Mrs. Elvsted, and Susan Colverd

Above all, Thea is devoted, her desertion of her oafish step-family not withstanding. Her loyalty to Lovborg inspires her to work with George Tesman to reconstruct Eilert's manuscript, their "child," which, she believes, Lovborg destroyed before his death. That Hedda is excluded from participating in their work contributes to Hedda's despair and suicide.

Hedda Gabler

Hedda is a complex character torn by opposing desires that make her both victim and victimizer. Her willfulness completely dominates the play, so much so that the other characters, even the more intriguing ones—Eilert Lovborg and Judge Brack seem to exist primarily to help sculpt her character in high relief.

Hedda is selfish, proud, and cold, cruelly heedless of the pain she inflicts on others in her efforts to satisfy the inner desires that she is unwilling to deal with honestly or directly. Inhibited by her upbringing, she is unwilling to sacrifice her own comfort to satisfy those longings, even though she finds her respectable marriage wearisome and her doting husband contemptible. Instead of dealing openly with her dissatisfaction and her growing fear of drowning in boredom, she becomes desperate, even hysterical, as is revealed in her sometimes treacherous and destructive behavior.

First of all, she rejects George's efforts to bring her closer to his family. In fact, from the start, she seems bent on ruining George's ties to his past. She refuses to address his Aunt Juliana with the familiar form of the pronoun "you" and, instead, treats her rudely. She also threatens to dismiss Berta, the loyal family servant. But her calculated coldness towards the Tesmans is most pronounced in her total lack of concern for George's Aunt Rina, whose death seems to affect Hedda not at all.

Secondly, Hedda responds only negatively to her new role as wife. Most particularly, she refuses to accept her own pregnancy, something in which she is unable to take any joy at all. She seems to sense that a child will forever bind her to a life of suffocating boredom. At best, marriage seems only to offer her a sort of sanctuary from a far more exciting but dangerous world beyond, the world of Eilert Lovborg, a world that she perceives as romantic and beautiful but also terrifying. She does not love George, and she deeply resents having to rely on him for security, but she has almost a parasitical need for his respectability.

Thirdly, Hedda attempts to manipulate others, either from spite or to satisfy her needs vicariously. The doting George is an easy pawn in Hedda's cruel games. So is Thea Elvsted, a woman too trusting of Hedda's seeming good will. Hedda's jealousy of Thea, a feeling that extends back into their school days, makes her betray the woman's confidence, setting in motion the tragedy that at the last will destroy both Lovborg and Hedda. It particularly goads Hedda that Thea has played a major role in Eilert's reclamation, corralling his free spirit and directing his energies in a way she herself was unable or unwilling to do. Her dislike of Thea goes yet deeper, however. Thea, as her appearance suggests, is warm and engaging, even sensual, whereas Hedda, though attractive, is steely and distant. Thea's large, blue eyes are fixed with "an inquiring expression," while Hedda's "steel-grey eyes express a cold, unruffled repose." Most especially, Hedda is obsessed with Thea's luxuriant and abundant hair, which she treats like a hated thing to be destroyed, almost as if it were a reminder of the passion that, from fear, she represses in herself. Her own hair is described by Ibsen as "not particularly abundant."

As long as Hedda is able to manipulate others, she can deal with her dangerous passions, including her sexuality. She had once driven Eilert off, threatening him with her father's pistols, and she threatens Brack in the same way. However, her options run out when Brack gets her in a compromising position, one in which she can be manipulated, something that she will not endure. Her only alternative is to take her own life.

While it is impossible to excuse Hedda's selfish and destructive character, at least some of the blame for her behavior rests with external influences, particularly her upbringing and the social dictates of her age. As the daughter of a general, she had learned to shoot and ride—hard, masculine activities that did not fit a respectable woman's role. That she is unable to make a mature adjustment to a feminine role, surrendering her freedom, is not entirely her fault.

Aunt Julia

See Miss Juliana Tesman

Eilert Lovborg

Eilert Lovborg is George Tesman's potential nemesis. Unlike Tesman, he is both a visionary and genius, but he is cursed with an inability to moderate his behavior. He carries disreputability on his back, luggage from a past in which he ruined his reputation by unspecified but dissolute conduct. However, when he first appears, he has renewed hopes. He has been inspired by Thea Elvsted, who has both prompted his reformation and been his able assistant in his scholarship and writing. He has also published a successful book and is close to finishing its more brilliant sequel.

Newly arrived in Christiania, Lovborg hopes to befriend George and interest him in his work, even though he is a threat to Tesman. He also attempts to refrain from any activity that might lead to a lapse into scandalous activity. However, his reformation proves both fragile and tragic when Hedda, his old love, reveals to him that Thea lacks sufficient faith in his self-control. He begins drinking, then goes off to Judge Brack's party. In the early morning, after heavy imbibing, he carelessly drops his manuscript on the street, where Tesman picks it up. It is later destroyed by Hedda, leading to Eilert's death and her own.

Lovborg offers a sharp contrast to Tesman. He is a disreputable and somewhat jaded genius, whereas George is a totally respectable and ingenuous plodder. Eilert has a creative, moody, and somewhat arrogant spirit; Tesman is unimaginative but steady and diligent. Hedda finds the latter boring but safe, and the former exciting but threatening.

Mrs. Rysing

See Mrs. Elvsted

George Tesman

George Tesman is a well-intentioned young man on his way to becoming a harmless drudge. He is a research scholar whose chief abilities, "collecting and arranging," are more clerical than insightful. He also seems more devoted to the minutia of history, the domestic industries of medieval Brabant, than he is to his wife, Hedda, around whom he usually seems doltish and imperceptive. He is unaware, for example, that she is pregnant, a fact that does not escape his Aunt Juliana. He also seems insensitive to Hedda's incivility and sarcasm, as well as her obvious discontent and bitterness.

On the other hand, George is devoted to his aunts, especially Juliana, who has been like a surrogate mother to him. He cares for her deeply, and he is upset that Hedda finds herself unable to develop a familiar relationship with her. To Hedda, Juliana is too much a busybody and too cloying in her affection.

Although professionally ambitious, Tesman is also essentially honest and fair. He recognizes in Lovborg the visionary genius that he utterly lacks, knowing, for example, that he could never make projections about the future the way Eilert has done in his manuscript sequel to his successful book. At the end of the play, he is willing to put aside his own work to collaborate with Mrs. Elvsted in an effort to reconstruct Lovborg's destroyed manuscript.

Tesman both bores and annoys Hedda. He treats life like his work, unimaginatively. At times he acts like a nincompoop, especially in his habit of responding to the most serious turn of events with the same inane enthusiasm accorded matters of no consequence. His tag expression, "fancy that," registers his apparently equal astonishment at the fact that his aunt has bought a new bonnet as, at the end, the fact that Hedda has shot and killed herself.

Hedda Tesman

See Hedda Gabler

Miss Juliana Tesman

Juliana Tesman, George Tesman's maiden aunt, has a deep affection for her nephew, who regards her with equal fondness. She is, in fact, a parental figure for Tesman, who calls her "father and mother in one" to him.

Juliana, who is sixty-five, is also devoted to her sister, George's Aunt Rina, who is an invalid. Juliana selflessly cares for her, and when she dies, Juliana immediately starts thinking about taking in an invalid boarder whom she might nurse. Her life, in short, is given over to ministering to the needs of others. She is the quintessential nurse, willing to sacrifice herself for others. Only in that does she find much meaning in life. In this respect, and in most others, she is a stark contrast to Hedda, who detests her.

Thea

See Mrs. Elvsted

Themes

Betrayal

At a critical point near the end of Act II of *Hedda Gabler*, the titular character betrays the trust of Mrs. Elvsted by revealing Thea's fears regarding Lovborg. Hedda does this out of pure malice. She is jealous of Thea's influence over Eilert, a man with whom Hedda had once been involved but, afraid of her own passions, had driven off (at gunpoint). Hedda's betrayal is the last manifestation of a hatred that extends all the way back to her school years, when she had bullied Thea. She despised the younger woman from a deep-rooted jealousy of Thea's comfortable and natural femininity. The betrayal starts a chain of tragic events in motion, ultimately leading to Lovborg's death and Hedda's suicide.

Courage and Cowardice

One admission that Hedda openly makes to Lovborg is her fear of scandal, which prompts him to charge that she is a "coward at heart," which she confirms. It was her fear of scandal that compelled Hedda to drive Eilert away, a fear that overwhelmed her love for him. Lovborg, as a free spirit, had represented too much of a risk, for he had already been tainted by his scandalous, immoderate behavior.

Although she, unlike Thea Elvsted, is unwilling to be drawn into Eilert's life again, to sacrifice her respectability, she is willing to sacrifice him. She provides him with a pistol, expecting him to exit life with a grand and triumphant display of scorn for the tedium and convention of human existence. From his death, Hedda hopes to confirm that there is still beauty in the world and partake of it vicariously. She is, however, deluded by her romantic fantasies, even less capable of guiding Eilert's behavior than Thea Elvsted had been. He destroys Hedda's triumphant vision by accidently shooting himself in the abdomen. In the play's final irony, it is Hedda who shoots herself in the temple, not in a grand escape from life but from a cowardly fear of scandal and an unwillingness to become Judge Brack's sexual pawn.

Topics for Further Study

- Investigate the influence of Ibsen's drama on the women's rights and emancipation movements of his day.

- Investigate "Ibsenism" in England in the last two decades of the nineteenth century, especially the dramatist's influence on Eleanor Marx (Karl Marx's youngest daughter), William Archer, and George Bernard Shaw.

- Research realism and naturalism as literary movements of the late-nineteenth century, relating their tenets to Ibsen's dramatic technique and themes in *Hedda Gabler*. You may want to consider reading Emile Zola's celebrated essay "Naturalism in the Theatre" (1880) in your investigation.

- Much modern drama reflects the strong influence of Henrik Ibsen, Anton Chekhov, and August Strindberg. Investigate and compare their particular contributions to the development of twentieth-century theater.

- Research the official morality of Ibsen's day that led to his notoriety and the condemnation and censorship of his plays, especially *Ghosts* and *Hedda Gabler*.

Deception

Hedda, from selfish motives, uses deception as a tool in her efforts to manipulate others, particularly her husband and Mrs. Elvsted. Because they are both forthright and somewhat ingenuous, they are susceptible to Hedda's machinations. Hedda feigns a friendship with Thea, one that she does not and never has felt. She is, in fact, jealous of the younger woman and despises her. In her relationship with George, Hedda never has been honest. She finds him and their marriage boring, but she is unwilling to confront him with such truths for fear of losing the secure respectability that he provides. He is, as she says, "correctness itself." He is also a man with good if dull prospects.

Hedda is more open with Judge Brack, possibly because she recognizes in him a kindred spirit, a fellow deceiver, one who is too sly to fool. She knows that Brack's friendship with George is at least part sham. He also hopes to manipulate Tesman, ingratiating himself in order to enter a triangular relationship with the Tesmans, which, through innuendo, Brack suggests will involve more than a Platonic friendship with Hedda. She is able to play a verbal cat and mouse game with Brack until he gains the upper hand; it is the prospect of submitting to his will that compels her to destroy herself.

Duty and Responsibility

Hedda Gabler is a study in contrasts. Both Juliana Tesman and Thea Elvsted are foils to Hedda, for in their distinct ways they reveal that duty and responsibility must arise from a loyalty prompted by love, not fear. Unlike Hedda, Juliana is a selfless person, willing to sacrifice her life for those she loves: her sister, Rina, and her nephew, George. She profoundly annoys Hedda, who cannot understand how such devotion can give Juliana a sufficient purpose in life.

Thea Elvsted has a similar selflessness, but her circumstances are very different. She is willing to sacrifice her reputation in her love for Lovborg, leaving behind a loveless, joyless marriage. Society might condemn her for betraying her duty and responsibility, but Ibsen makes it obvious that society would be wrong. She had been exploited, turned into a mere household servant in her marriage to the Sheriff. In following Lovborg to Christiania, Thea is heedless of imminent scandal, showing the moral courage that Hedda lacks. The difference is that Thea allows love to guide her, an emotion that Hedda represses in allowing her fears to rule her.

Good and Evil

"Evil" is too strong an adjective to apply to Hedda in any absolute sense. She does exhibit self-centered traits, as do most intriguing, dramatic villains, but these tendencies are muted by the playwright's dedication to realism. Hedda's wretched behavior cannot be forgiven, but at least it can be partially understood. It comes not from the deep recesses of a corrupt soul but from emotional needs that have been warped by environmental influences—her upbringing by a military father and her context within a morally strict social climate.

Despite this background, Hedda is proud and wanton in her cruelty. She cares little that she inflicts pain on others. She burns Lovborg's manuscript, not from love for her husband, which she leads George to believe, but from utter spite and jealousy. She views the work as Eilert and Thea's surrogate child, something to be destroyed because it was created from a love that she deeply resents and cannot understand. No less vicious is her effort to shape Eilert's final destiny, the "beautiful" and "triumphant" death she envisions for him. Her misdirected passion only destroys, for in Eilert's death there is no beauty at all, only a terrible waste of genius.

The shame is that to be good in Hedda's terms means living with unrelieved boredom, married to a "proper" but dull, plodding, and predictable scholar whose only virtue is his "correctness" in all things. Without real love or devotion, her duties and responsibilities become major irritants. She reacts with precipitous and thoughtless behavior, running the gamut between the petty and the tragic.

Sex Roles

Much of the conflict in *Hedda Gabler* arises from Hedda's resistance to the role of wife and mother, a role defined by the straight-laced, paternalistic society of the time and place. Women were expected to behave in accordance with traditional values that placed them in subservient and dependant relationships with men, from whose labors and leisure activities, both by custom and law, they were largely excluded. One hope they might have is that they could have a positive influence on men, such as Thea Elvsted has on Eilert Lovborg. Hedda even imagines that she might have a similar impact on George. She hopes to persuade him to enter politics, where, because of her ability to manipulate him, she might yield some clandestine but substantial power. However, when she confides her hopes in Judge Brack, he dampens her enthusiasm with observations about George's unsuitability for and disinterest in politics.

Hedda clearly feels both trapped and bored by her role. Her unwanted pregnancy only serves to remind her of just how much more confining her existence is to become, but she is paralyzed by her deep-rooted fear of scandal. She is simply unwilling to sacrifice respectability to be her honest self. The conflict between desire and fear finally perverts her character, turning her increasingly frantic and destructive. Her only respite is to cling to her father's pistols, symbols of a male freedom that she has lost as an adult and can never regain.

By contrast, Juliana Tesman and Thea Elvsted are comfortable and untroubled in their roles.

Juliana, as nurse and caretaker for her sister, is selfless. Her respectable role is personally rewarding. Thea, who has sacrificed her reputation by abandoning her husband, is untroubled by such things. She sees that her path lies outside of respectability, and she is not afraid to follow it. Hedda scorns both women, masking her envy with contempt. It galls her that they are both at peace with themselves, something she can never be.

Victim and Victimization

Paradoxically, Hedda is both victim and victimizer. In her desperate boredom, she attempts to use others, even for petty amusement. As she confesses to Judge Brack, she had known that the bonnet about which she complains in Act I was not old and did not belong to Berta, but she could not resist her cruel whimsy. At first, there is little harm done. Besides, Hedda's discontent enlists some sympathy, for her husband is something of a ninny, who, for all his doting behavior, is all but oblivious of her needs.

Hedda must bear the responsibility for the marriage, however. As she acknowledges, she had been the one to fashion it, not from love, but from her need for comfort and respectability. That she cannot abide either her husband or her marriage is her own fault, and in that sense she is her own victim. She responds with anger and resentment, taking her desperation out on others, those she envies because they have found a contentment that completely eludes her.

At the same time, Hedda is very vulnerable. The fears that had led her to reject Eilert Lovborg and enter a loveless marriage with George Tesman finally ensnare her in Brack's power, something that she can not tolerate. The alternative is scandal, which Hedda elects to evade by suicide, her final destructive act.

Style

Setting

While it is important, the physical setting of *Hedda Gabler*—the Tesmans' newly purchased villa in Christiania, Norway—is of less importance than the social environment of the time and place. The comfortably furnished house reflects both the class status of the Tesmans and their future expectations. In the first act, Hedda makes it clear that they plan to move beyond mere comfort to new levels of luxury. Her old piano, unsuited for the drawing room decor, must be moved into another room, to be replaced by a second, more elegant piano—at best a frivolous and impractical expense. Hedda wants both the security of respectability and the extravagant lifestyle of the wealthy, something threatened by Lovborg's arrival.

There is a price to be paid, though, a price that makes the villa a kind of prison. Against her innermost desires, Hedda must act like a proper wife, deferring to her husband's authority. She attempts to feign that role, but she finds it extremely boring. She grows desperate, especially when George warns that his appointment is no certainty. Fearing the loss of comfort as much as the loss of respectability, Hedda destroys Eilert's manuscript and bamboozles George into believing that she did it out of love for him. Hedda will not live in such a cage unless it is extremely well-appointed and all her material needs are met. She is simply that selfish and abusive of others.

Structure

Hedda Gabler, a four-act play, has what at the time was probably the most common formal pattern of dividing full-length plays into discrete segments. Works from earlier eras are usually divided into five acts, while more modern plays are generally divided into either three acts or, as is the case with many contemporary plays, into two acts. As is also traditional, the acts of *Hedda Gabler* mark divisions in time, segments in which significant action occurs over the course of two days. The plot is linear in its progression, strictly adhering to a straight-forward, chronological order.

Equally important, each act reaches a climactic moment when something decisive or irreversible is said or done. These are memorable moments, when, for example, at the end of the second act, Hedda burns Eilert's manuscript or, at the end of the play, kills herself with one of her father's pistols. Each act has the classic dramatic structure characterizing the play as a whole, and the warp and woof of each is a rising action that takes the whole to a new plateau of tension. In short, *Hedda Gabler*, provides an excellent example of what constitutes "a well-made play."

Realism

Like the other social-problem or thesis plays of Ibsen, *Hedda Gabler* follows the tenets of realism prevalent in late nineteenth-century Europe. Principal among these was the idea that the writer should render life both objectively and faithfully, concentrating on fairly ordinary people who face problems that can only be resolved in a manner that is true to life. In his realistic works, Ibsen sought to capture a sense of reality by using the characteristics of ordinary conversation, unencumbered with ornate diction and insistent poetic effects. In their cadences and diction his characters speak like real people, if, from dramatic necessity, somewhat more effortlessly and pointedly, and, in Norwegian at least, somewhat more sonorously.

Generally, too, characters in such works have discernible and valid motives for their behavior, even if they are complex, as they are in Hedda's case. If they are not clear, they must at least have verisimilitude, that quality that allows the viewer to conclude that even very puzzling characters are true to life and have validity. Ibsen allows his audience glimpses into Hedda's deeper motives, those things which do not wholly surface in the play's verbal matrix but are suggested, for example, both in persistent symbols and in her actions.

It is in *Hedda Gabler* that Ibsen takes his realism in drama to his limits. It has been described as the dramatist's most objective work, almost clinical in its coldness and distance. His plot driver, Hedda, is a vicious, petty, and extremely selfish woman, for whom, in Ibsen's time, few could find an iota of sympathy. Perhaps to underscore her brusque incivility and abrupt mood changes, Ibsen experimented with a new technique, eliminating long speeches altogether. He also used insistent words and phrases to reveal and even encapsulate his characters, a prime example being the "fancy that" of George Tesman.

Foil

An important device used by Ibsen in *Hedda Gabler* is the character foil. Contrasting figures help define their counterparts, providing a heightened sense of each character's personality. Hedda has two principal foils: Thea Elvsted and Juliana Tesman. Both women are very unselfish and at peace with life, willing to sacrifice themselves for others, even though, in Thea's case, it will destroy her reputation. Hedda's paralyzing fear of losing respectability stands in sharp contrast.

George Tesman and Eilert Lovborg are also foils. Tesman is "correctness" itself, a dull but steady plodder with a very limited imagination. His principal interest as scholar lies in rooting through the relics of the past, taking and organizing notes about the domestic industries of medieval Brabant. Lovborg, in contrast, is an erratic genius, prone to excess and easily drawn to hedonistic pleasures. As a visionary scholar, he is much more interested in the past for what it may reveal about the future, the unknown. He is, however, arrogant, self-destructive, and, at the last, somewhat pathetic.

Symbol

Ibsen makes it impossible to ignore some important symbols in *Hedda Gabler*. Primary are the pistols, Thea Elvsted's hair, and Eilert's manuscript. Because of the association made by both Hedda and Thea, the most obvious of these is Lovborg's manuscript. In the minds of both, the work is Eilert and Thea's "child," born of their love and affection for each other. It is partly from her intense jealousy that Hedda destroys it and sets out to break the bond between Thea and Lovborg.

Less open in symbolic significance is Thea's luxurious and abundant hair, especially as it contrasts with Hedda's own. Thea's hair is a point of fixation for Hedda, something that she despised in Thea when the two were schoolgirls; it continues to annoy her during the course of the play. Thea's hair seems to embody those qualities in Thea's character that Hedda lacks, including an engaging femininity that Hedda envies, perhaps even a sensuality that Hedda hates because she represses it in herself.

The pistols, on the other hand, suggest masculinity, and have long been identified as phallic symbols. It is noteworthy that both George Tesman and Judge Brack are appalled by the fact that Hedda plays with them. As extensions of Hedda's character, the guns suggest a masculinity, a hardening that has resulted from her repressed femininity. They represent the freedom that Hedda longs for but must sacrifice to respectability.

Historical Context

When Ibsen returned to his native Norway in 1891, he journeyed to a land that to a great degree was isolated from the revolutionary movements affecting both society and culture in the more cosmopolitan centers of Europe. That isolation was partly the result of inaccessibility. Modern communication and transportation were still in their infancy, awaiting the second major stage of the industrial revolution. The post and telegraph were the only real means of exchanging information over long distances, for the telephone was not yet in general use and wireless or radio communications were still the yet-to-be-realized dreams of Guglielmo Marconi and other inventors and engineers.

But Norway was also isolated in other ways. The dominate religion, Evangelical Lutheranism, was a conservative force in the social thinking of the country and one that, through his creative life, had not treated Ibsen well. The dramatist's frank treatment of taboo subjects and rigorous scrutiny of traditional mores offended many of his straightlaced countrymen. As a result, Ibsen was forced into a long artistic exile from his homeland.

A continent away, in the United States, as the historian Frederick Jackson Turner noted, the frontier was finally closing. In 1890, the last great Indian uprising was savagely crushed at the Battle of Wounded Knee, South Dakota, the final brutal "taming" of the West. The United States would soon look across the seas for new challenges and new opportunities.

Meanwhile, the British Empire was still in a major stage of development, making inroads in the near and far East by dint of its superior naval power. Indeed, it ruled the seas, though in Africa and other undeveloped areas of the world it had major competitors, including Germany and France, which, like Great Britain, looked for raw materials and markets to exploit.

The seeds of more revolutionary changes were also sown in the 1890s. By the middle of the decade, Sigmund Freud had begun developing his psychoanalytical method, Louis and Auguste Lumière had introduced moving pictures, William Roentgen had discovered X-rays, and Joseph Thomson had isolated the electron. The world was still reeling from the influence of two important thinkers, Karl Marx and Charles Darwin, whose impact was being felt in everything from religion and politics to arts and letters. Marx's theories of group ownership and a government run by the people were the first seeds of the communist movement that would later sweep across Eastern Europe and Asia. Darwin's theories of evolution challenged the religious notions of immaculate conception and divine spark. Great changes were underway, and they were coming at a rate never before experienced.

Compare & Contrast

- **1890s:** The world stands on the threshold of the second major phase of the industrial revolution, revolutionary changes in communications and transportation, the advent of the automobile, airplane, radio, phonograph, and film. These innovations will bring isolated communities into virtual proximity with the cultural and political centers of the world.

  Today: In the advanced nations of the world, the industrial revolution has ended. It is the time of technological revolution, leading the world into the space and information ages. Satellite communications and the computer make it possible for even the most isolated people to communicate with anyone in the world.

- **1890s:** Puritanical codes of acceptable behavior govern the social mores of Ibsen's day. Throughout Europe, social sanctions against such things as pre-marital sex, divorce, and family abandonment are strong, forcing many people to live miserable lives.

The so-called "Victorian underground" teems with prostitutes and thieves, many of whom are "fallen women" who had to resort to such a life or face abject poverty. Officially, however, moral sanctions in society were strict and penalties for infractions severe.

Today: Life in most post-industrial societies is permissive. In the United States, many marriages end in divorce. In many urban areas, single-parent families are prevalent, with pregnancy among unmarried teenage girls reaching epidemic proportions, despite the availability of birth-control drugs and devices. Homosexuality has not only been decriminalized, it has reached considerably wide acceptance, at least in some quarters. The overall nature of this "non-taboo" society has led many conservatives to call for a return to "family values" and the respectable morality of Ibsen's day.

- **1890s:** Official and unofficial protectors of the strict community moral standards put theatrical performances under close scrutiny, and many have the authority either to shut down productions or lead boycotts or protests, some of which result in riots. Plays can even be censored before they are performed.

Today: Both on stage and in media, especially film, there is virtually no official censorship. In the United States, for example, whatever moral codes relate to the substance of produced and broadcast works are self-imposed by the industries themselves. Frank treatment of what were once considered indelicate subjects is common, as are nudity, sex, and violence. Only the boycott remains as a possible avenue of protest, and it is rarely effective.

- **1890s:** In Ibsen's day, men and women live separate lives. Although there are various women's organizations dedicated to change, women remain "unliberated," except, perhaps, in groups on the fringes of respectable society. They are educated in their own finishing schools and are excluded from most professions. Much of their leisure time is spent in the company of other women, segregated from men. They lack political power because, even in the democracies, they lack the vote. Their possibilities in life outside of marriage are limited, unless, like *Mme.* Diana in Ibsen's play, they are willing to sacrifice their reputations.

Today: Although many feminists still argue that women have yet to complete their liberation, enfranchisement and greater freedom have resulted from the revolutionary changes that have occurred in this century. Women who sacrifice marriage and family for a career still earn reproach from more reactionary corners, but they are hardly censured or demonized by society at large. There remain few male-only bastions, and these are all under siege, at least in the United States. Women take the same jobs as men, go to the same schools, study the same subjects, and mix freely with men at all functions, from corporate board meetings to sporting events. The feminist complaints of today are not so much about exclusion now as they are about equal treatment and compensation.

In the last decade of the nineteenth century, *fin de siecle* ("end of the century") artists were selfconsciously abandoning traditional and conventional forms and techniques in favor of more experimental ones. It was a complex period of transition, having as one of its maxims "art for art's sake." It also reflected the new philosophies that called so much into doubt. The naturalistic school, for example, viewed humanity on the lower end of the socioeconomic ladder, trapped there by environmental forces beyond its control.

Two *fin de siecle* British writers of importance were Oscar Wilde (*The Importance of Being Earnest*) and George Bernard Shaw (*Man and Superman*), both of whom wrote plays. Shaw was Ibsen's bulldog in England, his great apologist and advocate. In the course of his own long life, he would become the greatest British dramatist of his age, and, next to Shakespeare, the second greatest in the history of British theater.

Critical Overview

Hedda Gabler was published in December of 1890, a few weeks before it was first performed. Norwegian, English, German, French, Russian, and Dutch versions were printed almost simultaneously, with the result that the consternation many readers felt quickly spread throughout Europe. The play garnered the worst press reviews of any of Ibsen's mature plays, even *Rosmersholm*, which had been critically mauled four years earlier. The newer work offended many and puzzled more critics, who, as Hans Heiberg noted in *Ibsen: A Portrait of the Artist*, found the main character too monstrous, a "revolting female creature" who "received neither sympathy nor compassion." Just as damning, the work seemed to lack a message, a corrective purpose, the sort of social critique for which Ibsen had become so famous.

Hedda's character was the principal target of much of the negative criticism. Quoted in *Ibsen: A Biography*, Alfred Sinding-Larsen called her "a horrid miscarriage of the imagination, a monster in female form to whom no parallel can be found in real life," suggesting that the great realist had completely missed the mark in creating her and that he was only "pandering to contemporary European fashion." Similar complaints came from even the most ardent admirers of Ibsen, including Bredo Morgenstierne. Reprinted in *Ibsen*, the critic opined: "we do not understand Hedda Gabler, nor believe in her. She is not related to anyone we know." Also quoted in *Ibsen*, Gerhard Gran observed that while the play aroused his curiosity, it did not and never could satisfy it. For Gran, a figure as complex as Hedda was not suited to drama and could only be satisfactorily treated in the novel; the play, he argued, only "leaves us with a sense of emptiness and betrayal."

Much of the criticism was lodged on moral grounds, renewed objections that Ibsen had faced with earlier plays like *A Doll's House* (1879) and *Ghosts* (1881). Some Scandinavian critics suggested that the printed play "should not be found on the table of any decent family." Others dismissed the work as either too puzzling or too decadent. Harald Hansen, reviewing stage productions of 1891, dismissed it in as single sentence as "an ungrateful play which hardly any of the participants will remember with real satisfaction" (*Ibsen*).

Ibsen and his play had their champions, including Henrik Jæger in Norway and Herman Bang in Denmark. Jæger, who had once gone on tour lecturing against A *Doll's House*, had become a pro-Ibsen convert. He saw Hedda as a very realistic, earth-born female, "a tragic character who is destroyed by the unharmonious and irreconcilable contrasts in her own character" (*Ibsen*). He suggested that the poor reception of *Hedda Gabler* stemmed from the general unpopularity of tragedy, not from faults in the play. Meanwhile, Bang, in some of the play's most perceptive early criticism, argued that Hedda was the female counterpart of a familiar Ibsen character, the egotistical male. Without the socially-sanctioned outlets afforded men, she is driven "into isolation and self-adoration." "Hedda," Bang observed, "has no source of richness in herself and must constantly seek it in others, so that her life becomes a pursuit of sensation and experiment; and her hatred of bearing a child is the ultimate expression of her egotism, the sickness that brings death" (*Ibsen*).

Most criticism, both of the printed play and first staged productions, was hostile, which, in retrospect, suggests a remarkable short-sightedness on the part of Ibsen's contemporaries. Now, over a century later, *Hedda Gabler* is considered one of the principal stars in the dramatist's artistic crown, and it has been for some time. In his 1971 biography *Ibsen*, Michael Meyer said that the work was then "perhaps the most universally admired of Ibsen's plays," and noted that it was Ibsen's most frequently performed work in England. Today, its chief competitor in Ibsen revivals is *A Doll's House*, in part because of its protagonist Nora Helmer's appeal to the women's liberation movement. Unlike Hedda, there is nothing vicious about Nora, who is mostly pure victim in a society under male control.

Interestingly enough, it is because Hedda so completely dominates her play that her role soon became very attractive to actresses, and because it proved a great vehicle for the most talented and highly regarded among them, it evolved from its maligned beginning into a stage favorite. Among those who undertook the role were leading international stars, including Eleonora Duse, Eve Le Gallienne, Nazimova, Mrs. Patrick Campbell, Claire Bloom, Joan Greenwood, Ingrid Bergman, and Glenda Jackson. That is the final irony, for it was the "monstrous" Hedda who, in the minds of the early critics, condemned the play, whereas it is now her character that makes it one of Ibsen's most durable works. The attraction of the part remains, despite the fact that the society that the play depicts is virtually extinct.

Sources

Finney, Gail. "Ibsen and Femininism" in *The Cambridge Companion to Ibsen*, edited by James McFarlane, Cambridge University Press, pp. 99-100.

Heiberg, Hans. *Ibsen: A Portrait of the Artist*, University of Miami Press, 1967, p. 257.

Weigand, Herman J. *The Modern Ibsen: A Reconsideration*, Books for Libraries Press, 1970, p. 242.

Further Reading

Barranger, Milly S. *Barron's Simplified Approach to Henrik Ibsen*, Barron's Educational Series, 1969.

> This brief monograph offers uncomplicated readings of *Hedda Gabler* and two other major Ibsen plays: *The Wild Duck* and *Ghosts*. It is a helpful guide to interpretation focusing on character, themes, and dramatic technique.

Durbach, Errol. *Ibsen the Romantic: Analogues of Paradise in the Later Plays*, University of George Press, 1982.

> Durbach discusses the romantic and counter-romantic currents in Ibsen that underlies his characters' search for meaning, their efforts to redeem themselves from an inhibiting and stultifying, uncreative life. It is a search that can be destructive, as in Hedda's case.

Lyons, Charles R. Hedda Gabler: *Gender, Role, and World*, Twayne, 1990.

> Lyons discusses both the cultural and historical milieu of *Hedda Gabler*, then discusses the play as a kind of mimetic snapshot of human behavior caught in that historical matrix and

argues that reader responses should reflect that limitation.

McFarlane, James, editor. *The Cambridge Companion to Ibsen*, Cambridge University Press, 1994.

> A collection of articles by contemporary scholars, this anthology includes important pieces on such topics as Ibsen's realistic problem plays, his relationship to feminism, and his impact on modern drama. The work includes helpful aids, including a chronology and notes on the first publication and performance of each of Ibsen's works.

Meyer, Michael. *Ibsen: A Biography*, Doubleday, 1971.

> A well-documented critical biography, this study makes extensive use of Ibsen's correspondence and summarizes the critical reception of his works in his own day.

Northam, John. *Ibsen's Dramatic Method: A Study of the Prose Dramas*, Universitetsforlaget, 1971.

> A recommended starting place for the study of Ibsen's technique, this work approaches the plays by analyzing the playwright's language

and its correlation with visual, on-stage images, as, for example, the opposing physical differences between Hedda and Thea Elvsted.

Young, Robert. *Time's Disinherited Children: Childhood, Regression, and Sacrifice in the Plays of Henrik Ibsen*, Norvik Press, 1989.

Young's central thesis is that the motives and needs of many of Ibsen's major characters reveal the disinherited child in the adult.

Lightning Source UK Ltd.
Milton Keynes UK
UKHW020712130622
404345UK00010B/1024